This book was published with the generous support of the Canada Council and the Ontario Arts Council.

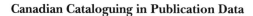

Canadian Cataloguing in Publication Data

Main entry under title:
Would you believe it?

ISBN 0-920775-52-7

1. Science — Miscellanea — Juvenile literature.
I. Farris, Katherine. II. Title: OWL magazine.

Q163.W68   1990   j500   C90-093764-5

Designer: Julie Colantonio
Cover Photograph: Nigel Dickson
Printed in Hong Kong

10 9 8 7 6 5 4 3 2 1

WOULD YOU BELIEVE IT?

From the Editors of OWL Magazine

Compiled and edited by Katherine Farris

Greey de Pencier Books

Does a baby hedgehog have spines?

Sometime from May to September, in Europe, Asia and Africa, baby hedgehogs are born in a safe, soft, warm, well-lined nest. At birth their eyes and ears are closed and they have no fur . . . they don't even have spines. Their spines are hidden just beneath the skin, which is swollen with fluid. This swelling prevents the spines from piercing the skin and hurting the mother during birth. Soon after birth, the fluid is absorbed by the baby's body and the 150 or so white spines poke through.

What animal has the most babies?

The house mouse takes the medal for the number of mammal babies: up to 32 in some litters. But that's nothing compared to the ocean sunfish, which lays up to 30 million eggs. Since the female just lays her eggs as she swims along and doesn't protect them, many of the eggs are eaten up by other fish. It's a good thing only a few ocean sunfish make it to adulthood. Why? Ocean sunfish are enormous, weighing up to 1,000 kg/2,200 lbs.

Why doesn't a baby kangaroo fall out of its mother's pouch?

A kangaroo's deep, upward-opening pouch is ideal for a hopping, grass-eating animal. The joey can't fall out no matter how fast its mother travels. And when the mother leans forward to graze, her baby can nibble on grass too, without even leaving the safety of her pouch! When the joey is about eight months old, its mother encourages it to get out and explore. She relaxes her pouch and out tumbles her baby. When the joey has had enough of the outside world, its mother spreads her legs, lowers her pouch, and her baby somersaults in headfirst.

How big is a baby elephant?

When it is born, a healthy male Sri Lankan elephant can weigh as much as 138 kg/304 lbs — that's heavier than the combined weight of more than 40 human babies. And that enormous size is matched by an unbelievable appetite. Baby elephants drink the equivalent of 15 large cartons of milk a day! With an appetite like that, it's no wonder the baby gains more than a kilo/2 ⅕ lbs every single day for the first little while. By the time it is one year old, it is four times heavier than it was at birth.

Do any animals give birth to identical twins?

Imagine the confusion that must face the nine-banded armadillo mother. Every spring, when she gives birth, she always has four identical babies that are all the same sex. At birth their skin is soft and leathery, but in a few weeks it hardens into bony body armor.

7

How do mice squeeze through such small holes?

A tiny house mouse has a sleek, small body, light, flexible bones and stretchy ligaments that let it scrunch, stretch and squeeze its body through holes smaller than a 25-cent piece!

Are mice always timid?

Most mice are quiet, gentle little creatures that prefer to avoid confrontations. But there are some mice that are so aggressive they might even scare off Mighty Mouse. They're known as grasshopper mice, and they live in the central and western regions of the U.S. They look like ordinary cute field mice, but they've earned the nickname of killer mice! These ferocious predators attack large insects, scorpions, even other mice — tearing them apart as they eat them. They even throw back their heads and pierce the air with their calls, just like wolves.

How can mice be so quiet?

Rubbery paws let the mouse pad silently around, its claws help it to grip surfaces, even very steep inclines, and its long, agile tail can be roped around a stem of grass or a wire to help the mouse keep its balance. And this can all be done with scarcely a rustle.

Why do mice have such big ears?

A mouse's large, round ears act like swiveling satellite dishes to help it pick up sounds from all directions. A mouse can hear many sounds we can't, especially high-frequency sounds. Excellent hearing helps the mouse avoid being snatched up by fast-flying birds. It's a good thing that mouse ears can hear so well because mouse eyes don't see very well.

Are mice really always busy?

Most mice scurry around day and night all year round, searching out food and exploring their territory, pausing only for naps. But dormice, which live in Europe and Asia, fatten up on food during the summer. When fall comes, they nestle into a safe hideout and hibernate until May.

How do mice see in the dark?

Mice are nearsighted, so they can distinguish something moving only if it's close by. In the dark, the mouse relies on its sensitive hearing and its sensitive whiskers. They let the mouse know how close it is to walls or other mice, or whether it will be able to squeeze through a small hole. Whiskers give the mouse a 3-D picture of the world in the dark.

Why can't fish close their eyes?

Fish don't have eyelids like yours. Your eyelids protect only when you blink or close your eyes to keep them wet and to wipe away dirt and dust and so on. That kind of protection isn't enough for a fish. Just as you put on a mask when you want to swim around and look at things underwater, so fish eyes have a clear covering that gives them constant protection.

Fish don't need eyelids like yours for other reasons. Since fish live in water their eyes are always wet. Also, things move more slowly in water than in air, so fish can dodge most dirt. And even if something does enter their eyes, it's not going fast enough to do much damage. To protect their eyes when they're racing towards their prey, sharks roll them back into their head, make a blind charge and, at the last second, unroll their eyes to see what's for dinner.

Why do some animals' eyes shine at night?

Animals that prowl around for food during the night need all the help they can get to be able to see. That's why most nocturnal, or night-active, mammals — such as deer, hyenas, skunks, porcupines, cats and dogs — have a shiny layer on the back inner surface of their eyes. This surface helps to reflect light back so the animal can see better in the dark. It's not just mammals that have this feature. Some species of fish, such as the tarpin, and some night-hunting spiders in Australia and Central and South America do too.

What animal has the biggest eyes in the world?

All squid have big eyes. But the rarely seen giant squid has eyes the size of an extra-large pizza. If you had eyes like the giant squid's, your face would have to be larger than a big wading pool to contain them. Talk about 20/20 vision!

How do fish see underwater?

It depends on the fish. Some fish use sunlight to see. In clear ocean waters, light can filter down to 300 m/1,000 ft. That's as deep as a 10-story building is tall! Other fish don't rely on sight. Instead they sense their environment, using whiskers, electric fields, smell and vibration.

How tall is a baby giraffe?

A newborn giraffe makes quite an entrance. Since the mother giraffe gives birth standing up, her calf literally drops into the world, falling 2 m/6 ½ ft. But even though it's about the same height and weight as a tall man, the calf is hidden away for a month or more. It reaches its full height by the time it's four, and continues to put on weight for another three or four years. For as long as it's still growing it's protected by adult giraffes.

What's the biggest fish in the world?

Would you believe that the biggest fish in the world is a shark that is harmless to humans? The whale shark may grow to be one and a half times the length of a bus, yet it eats only plankton and small fish. So even though its jaws hold up to 4,000 teeth, each tooth is so tiny the whale shark will never replace its great white cousin as a movie star!

What's the biggest bird that can fly?

The heaviest flying bird is the Kori bustard that soars through the skies of eastern and southern Africa. It weighs as much as an 11-kg/30-lb, three-year-old child.

How big is a giant panda?

A giant panda isn't really a giant. At birth it isn't much bigger than a mouse. And when it's full grown it weighs about as much as a big man and is only about 1 m/3 ft tall at the shoulder. But one thing about the panda is giant — its appetite for bamboo. It eats about 27 kg/60 lbs of it daily. No wonder the giant panda spends almost all of its waking hours eating.

What's the biggest bug?

First we should make something clear. A bug is a specific kind of insect that has a special front-wing structure and a beak-like tool that it uses for feeding. Other insects do not have these features. Some common bugs that you might have seen are bedbugs, stink bugs, water boatmen and water striders. (Ladybugs and mealybugs are *not* true bugs.)

The biggest bug is the giant water bug. Common in ponds across North America, this dark brown creature can grow to a length of just over 50 mm/2 in. The South American species is twice that length! The giant water bug gets that big by eating insects, snails, tadpoles and even small fish. It grabs them with its front legs, sticks in its beak and sucks out their juices.

When it's had enough of the water, the giant water bug spreads its wings and flies about. If you're lucky you might see one hovering around your porch light on a hot summer night.

By the way, the biggest flying *insect* is the Goliath beetle — it tips the scales at 100 g/3 ½ oz.

Why are babies so cute?

Babies' looks are designed to help them get what they want. That might sound strange to you, but since babies can't talk, they need other ways to tell their parents what they want or need. For example, a baby needs to be accepted and not ignored. Those huge eyes, full cheeks and tiny mouth and nose are so appealing and unthreatening that a parent will be sure to give the baby as much attention as possible.

A baby also needs to be stimulated to learn things. Having silky hair and soft skin invites a parent to stroke and groom the baby. In the process, the parent will probably also play with the baby.

A baby needs to be cuddled so that it knows it's safe. Its tiny round body feels wonderfully soft and warm. No wonder a parent delights in holding such a comforting bundle.

But looks aren't everything...

A baby doesn't rely on being cute to make adults want to look after it.
It has other ways to get adults to take care of its needs . . .

Why do babies cry?

I want something! If you've ever heard a baby crying, you know you'll do anything to get it to stop. A baby's cry is pitched at a level that most people can't tolerate for long. And because they find it so stressful to hear, most adults will pick up the crying baby and hold it, feed it, change its diaper or do whatever else it takes to make the baby happy.

If the cry doesn't work, a baby can try another tactic. It will cry and thrash about helplessly. Any adult who takes a look at a baby's tightly screwed-up, grimacing little face and helplessly thrashing arms and legs can't help but want to pick it up.

If a baby is suddenly startled or too roughly handled or played with, it will either cry or try to shut out the source of the alarm by closing its eyes tight, tensing its body and taking deep, ragged breaths. These clues help the baby's parents to know that whatever's happening is more than their baby can handle.

Pick Me Up!

If a baby sees its mother's face it stares intently at her: its eyes widen and its face softens and becomes more alert. The eye contact prompts the mother to stare back, make faces and just generally amuse the little one for as long as it is interested.

This kind of eye-to-eye contact helps to deepen the bond between the two. Sometimes the baby may even crane its neck as it lifts its chin towards her. When the mother sees the baby literally straining to make contact, she will immediately bend down to pick up her baby and cuddle it.

Hold Me More!

A baby even has ways to say it wants to be cuddled some more. If you've held a baby on your shoulder, you'll know that it will automatically turn towards your chest and mold its legs around your side. When the baby gets tired it will put its head against your shoulder and nestle into the crook of your neck. The feeling of the baby's soft little head resting against your neck is irresistible, and you'll cuddle it even more.

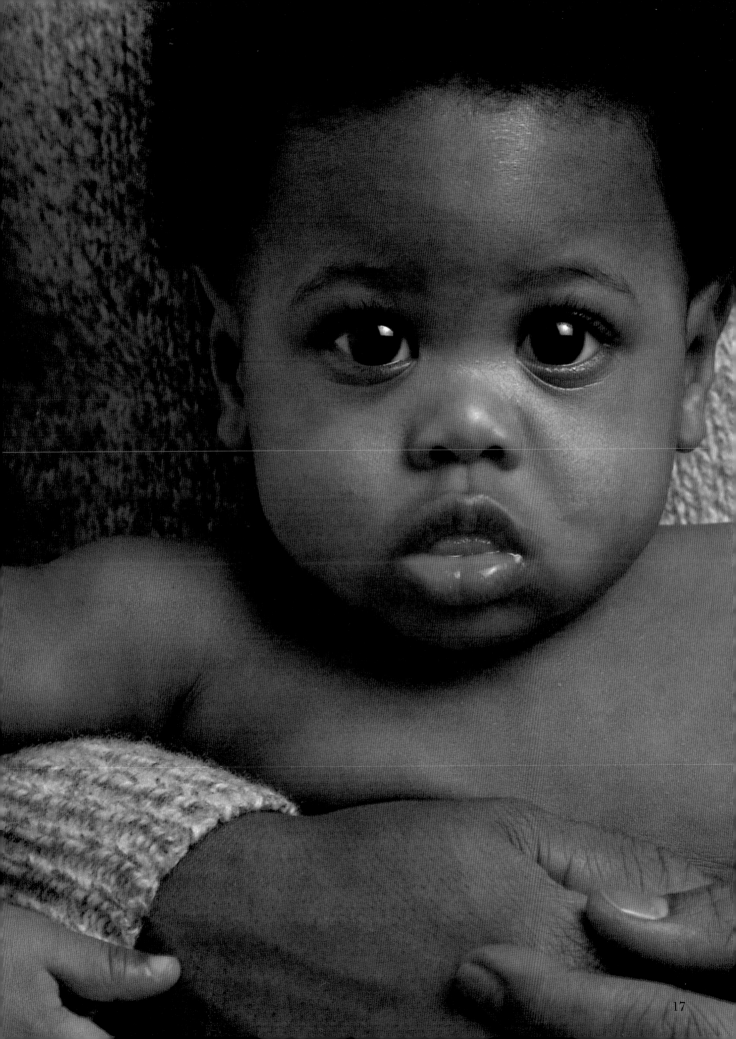
17

Why do elephants ▼ trumpet?

Elephants trumpet for the same reasons that you yell. They do it when they're excited, surprised or want to warn another elephant of danger. They also trumpet when they're lost or about to attack. Elephants communicate in other ways too. They let members of their herd know that they are near and everything is safe by producing low rumbles in their bellies. A female elephant may call her young to her by noisily slapping her ears against her head. And some scientists think that elephants can communicate with such low sounds that humans feel them rather than hear them. Next time you're at a zoo, try to listen in on an ultra-low elephant conversation.

Do prairie dogs really bark?

Yes. In fact, prairie dogs are one of the animal world's most precise communicators. If an eagle swoops overhead, for example, they use their bark to alert the rest of the town that danger is nearby. All the prairie dogs that hear the warning signal immediately dive underground. It's thought that prairie dogs give a different call for as many as nine different enemies. And barks aren't the only sound prairie dogs make. They chitter when they're frustrated or mad, they chuckle when they're happy, they scream in pain or fear and they snarl when they're fighting.

How do dolphins whistle?

Imagine talking through your nose! That's what the dolphin does. It breathes in air through its blowhole when it's at the surface. Then, when it wants to talk to other dolphins, it moves "lips" inside the blowhole and makes squeals, whistles and clicks.

Why do rabbits thump?

Did you ever wonder why Bambi's friend Thumper thumped? When rabbits, and for that matter some hares, sense danger, they thump with their king-sized feet probably to warn others.

Are March hares really mad?

The March hare in Alice in Wonderland might have been mad during the month of March, but most hares act crazy from March right through till May. That's the mating season. During that time the hares might fight. And that's not all. Their hopping, running and chasing antics are enough to make the March hare look sane!

What's the difference between hares and rabbits?

If you can't tell the difference between hares and rabbits, you're not alone. Here's how the experts know who's who. Hares tend to be bigger than rabbits and have longer ears and legs. Also, hares molt twice a year and change color, while rabbits never change color. Finally, at birth hare babies are covered with hair and can see. Rabbit babies, however, are born hairless and can't see at all. Got it now? Okay — who's in the picture at the right, a rabbit or a hare?

How fast can a rabbit run?

Hares are some of the speediest animals around. The white-tailed jackrabbit, which is actually a hare, can hit speeds of up to 72 km/h/45 mph for short periods. It can leap 6 m/20 ft straight up into the air to keep an eye on pursuing predators.

Why do rabbit tracks look as if they're going backwards?

Next time you see a rabbit running quickly, watch it carefully. First it puts its small front feet down, usually one in front of the other or sometimes side by side. Rabbits' front legs are great for helping it to keep balanced or change direction. But they're too short to keep up with its long back legs. So when a rabbit runs fast, its back legs overtake its front ones and its big hind paws thump the ground in front of them.

What is personal space?

◆ Just as animals have their territories to defend, so do people. Personal space is the space immediately surrounding you that you claim as your own. If anyone gets too close to you under the wrong circumstances, you feel uncomfortable because your personal space has been invaded.

Why do you have personal space?

Scientists still aren't sure why people have personal spaces. One idea is that it keeps you from bumping into people or having things spilled on you. Or perhaps keeping your distance helps slow down the spread of germs.

How big is your personal space?

If you could see your personal space, it would probably look something like a bulky spacesuit. It's a bit bigger in front of you than at your sides or behind you.

Whom you're with, where you are and what you're doing all help determine the size of your personal space. It "shrinks" when you're with people you like and trust.

How to find out the size of your personal space

1. In an open area, ask a friend to stand 2 m/7 ft away, facing you.

2. Tell her to look at your chin and walk slowly towards you, hands at her sides. She mustn't grin or make a face.

3. You should look at her eyes. When you feel uncomfortable about how close she is getting, say "stop."

4. Ask other friends to approach you in the same way. To find out your average personal space, divide the sum of all the distances by the number of people who approached you.

5. Ask your friends to do the same to find their average personal space.

Does your personal space change when you can't see?

Repeat the experiment that tests the size of your personal space, but blindfold yourself. As in the first experiment, have several kids approach you. The approachers must count as they walk towards you so you know where they are. Tell them to stop when you feel uncomfortable and measure the distance between you. Record these distances, then figure out your average "blindfolded" personal space. Is it different from the average with your eyes open? Ask the other kids to test their average "blindfolded" personal space.

What's the "Great Red Spot" on Jupiter?

In March 1979, the robot spacecrafts Voyager I and II began to send back to Earth pictures of Jupiter. These photographs revealed that one of the planet's biggest mysteries, the Great Red Spot, is a swirling hurricane three times larger than Earth. Some years the spot is bright red, and other years it's salmon colored. Scientists think the color change could be due to different amounts of red phosphorus.

Voyager also confirmed that Jupiter is a world of whirling clouds and poisonous gases. Great lightning storms rage around the planet and winds of up to 400 km/h /250 mph whip the clouds across the sky. Jupiter's very faint ring may have been created when a moon got too close and broke into small pieces.

Why is space so cold?

The space in between all those far-flung stars is mostly a big stretch of nothing, an airless vacuum. This means that there's not much dust or gas in space that could trap and hold the heat from all those stars. So the heat, in the form of radiation, simply keeps on traveling. Eventually the radiation strikes something big enough to absorb its heat, for instance planets and moons, but the space in between them never heats up. No one knows for sure, but scientists guess that the temperature in space could be as low as -273°C/ -459°F. Scientists call this absolute zero. It's certainly absolutely cold!

Why doesn't air leak into space?

Relax! Before anything can escape the tremendous pull of Earth's gravity, it must achieve a speed of 11 km/s or 7 miles per second! That's how fast the space shuttle leaves Earth, and that's the speed our air must achieve before it can escape into space. And that's not likely to happen. A hurricane blows only about 120 km/h/75 mph.

Can a jet fly into outer space?

What's to stop the fastest jet on Earth from flying up to the moon? Many things, just one being that as soon as the plane left Earth's atmosphere (assuming it could fly fast enough to escape Earth's gravity) its jet engines would die. That's because jet engines need oxygen to operate, and there isn't any oxygen in space. Without engine power, the plane would eventually be pulled back to Earth.

Why are there still footprints on the moon?

On July 20, 1969, millions of television viewers around the world watched spellbound as U.S. astronaut Neil Armstrong climbed down from the lunar module Eagle onto the dusty surface of the moon. Soon he was joined by Edwin (Buzz) Aldrin, Jr., and together they spent the next 21½ hours setting up experiments and bounding around like kangaroos in the weak lunar gravity. All those footprints they left — and those of later Apollo astronauts — are still there today, looking exactly as they did when they were first made. Why? The moon has no atmosphere so there is no wind or weather to blow or wash away the imprints of the first pairs of authentic moon boots. Tiny meteorites that constantly fall on the moon will eventually erode the footprints, but that will take millions of years.

Do animals get tanned? ▲

When they wake up on a bright sunny morning, most animals don't get out the beach towels and suntan lotion, because they are so furry they couldn't get a tan even if they wanted to. But some animals do lie around in the sun for other reasons.

Ring-tailed lemurs sunbathe in groups, before breakfast, standing up with their arms outstretched. They do it because they have poor blood circulation. If they didn't soak up the sun's warmth every morning, they would end up with a bad case of cold hands and feet.

To survive in the scorching desert heat, camels face into the sun whenever possible. That way the least possible amount of their body surface is exposed to the sun's burning rays.

Do animals get sunstroke?

Hot cows get cranky and can easily become sick. But finding shade on the prairies, where trees are scarce, can be a problem. To keep their cows cool, some prairie farmers wheel enormous slatted sunshades out into the fields. Although the slats let some sun through, they also allow the air to keep moving, which keeps the cows cool.

Can animals get sunburned?

Animals that don't have fur often need protection from the sun. Elephants, for example, go through a two-step process to prevent getting sunburned. After rolling in the mud they spray themselves with trunkfuls of dust. The dust sticks to the mud and protects the elephants' skin from the sun's harmful rays. It also makes a sandpaper coating that squishes unwanted bugs when the elephant rubs against a tree.

Why do racing cyclists bend so low over their handlebars?

How you sit on your bike affects how you battle the force of the wind. On some bikes you sit upright, which is good for comfort. But if you want speed, you have to lower both the handlebars and your shoulders. This makes your chest and shoulders a smaller target area for the wind so it can't push against you as hard and slow you down.

Racers crouch low on their bikes and wear smooth, tight-fitting suits and helmets with a tail so that the air will slide smoothly over them. Racing bikes also have enclosed wheels and frames to further reduce air resistance, adding a tiny bit of extra speed that just might be enough to win.

How do reflectors work?

Believe it or not, the design of the safety reflectors on a bicycle is similar to that of the retroreflectors left on the moon by the Apollo astronauts. Both reflectors contain tiny prisms that bounce light beams back to their source. On Earth, safety reflectors bounce car headlight beams straight back to the driver of the car. On the moon, retroreflectors bounce laser beams back to scientists on Earth. Why? By timing how long the beams take to travel there and back, they can measure the distance between the planet and its moon.

Why does your bicycle have gears?

Gears on your bike allow you to change your rate of pedaling while your wheels maintain their speed going up or down hills. What's the advantage in that? In low gear, your legs move quicker than your wheels, giving you many power strokes in a short distance to help you climb hills or drive through soft sand. High gear gives you many spins of the wheel for only a few strokes of your legs, so you can speed almost effortlessly downhill or along hard, level surfaces. Without gears on your bike, you'd have to pedal at the same speeds that your wheels were turning — wobblingly slow going uphill and furiously fast flying downhill.

● ● ● ● ● ● ● ● ● ●

Which are better, fat tires or thin ones?

It depends what you want to do with your bike. Fat tires spread out your weight over a large area. That's why you can ride a mountain bike over sand without sinking in. But as fat, squishy tires roll along, they come in contact with a wide strip of ground, which slows them down. It's known as rolling resistance. Racing tires, on the other hand, are thin and hard, so their contact area with the ground is as small as possible and you have very little resistance to overcome.

Why do you have to lean into a turn when you're biking?

Don't try turning a corner fast without leaning into it — you'll end up on the ground. You must lean into a turn to balance all the forces acting on your bike. At the beginning of the lean, your balancing point, known as your center of mass, is no longer over the wheels, so gravity begins to pull you down. At the same time, centripetal force, produced when your bike begins to turn, forces you towards the inside of the turn. Inertia comes to your rescue, however. This is the tendency of a moving object to keep moving in a straight line, and it's what pulls you towards the outside of the turn and balances the two other forces that pull you in and down.

Are all frogs green?

No. It's true that most frogs do have green markings, which they rely on for camouflage. But one small group of frogs are blue, orange, pink, yellow, red or brown. Why are they so brightly colored? It's their way of warning potential predators, such as birds, not to eat them.

This poison dart frog, for example, is so poisonous it doesn't need to hide from predators. In fact, no other animal produces a poison so deadly. Indians of Central and South America, where this frog lives, poison the tips of their hunting darts with the deadly secretions from its skin. That's how the frog gets its name.

Where do frogs lay their eggs?

Most frogs lay their eggs in water. However, some lay them on the ground, others lay them on leaves, and still others lay them underground. When it's time to lay their eggs, female African tree frogs select a branch over a pond or a swamp. Then they secrete a fluid, which the males help whip into a foam with their hind legs. After the females lay their eggs in this frothy nest, it forms a hard crust. A few weeks later the tadpoles break through the crust and drop to the water below.

Why do frogs croak?

Frogs croak to communicate . . . but not all frogs communicate by croaking. Some cluck, some bleat, some whistle, some scream. And the mating call of the male barking tree frog sounds more like a dog's bark than a croak. People claim that you can hear it 1.6 km/1 mile away! P.S. If you live or have traveled in the southern United States, you may have heard a barking tree frog. But unless you actually saw one, how would you know? Woof, woof.

Do all frogs live in ponds?

No. A few frogs live on the rain forest floor, others in sand dunes. The tree frog, however, leaves the pond it swam in as a tadpole and lives almost exclusively in . . . you guessed it, trees. The broad pads on its fingertips enable the frog to hold on tight so it can walk up tree trunks or hang from branches.

How do chameleons catch insects?

Unlike other lizards that usually chase after their prey, the chameleon slowly stalks the insects it eats for dinner. By creeping very slowly and changing its color to match the surrounding leaves, the chameleon avoids being spotted. When it gets about a body's length away from its meal, the chameleon suddenly flings out its long, slime-tipped tongue. The meal sticks to the tongue's tip and is then reeled in.

Why do slugs leave a trail of slime?

When a slug goes searching for juicy plants to eat, it glides on a trail of its own slime. How? The slug's long foot moves like a wave. When the slug puts down its "heel," the slime is sticky and glues the foot for take off. Then, as the foot ripples forward, the pressure causes the mucus-like slime to become more liquid and slippery so that the foot can slide along. Scientists are still baffled by how the slime changes back and forth from a solid to a liquid.

Why are fish slimy?

Without slime, fish would have a tough life. The water they swim in is full of parasites trying to latch on to any fish skin they can find. Slime to the rescue! It provides a shield that bacteria, fungi and algae can't penetrate. Fish continually secrete and shed slime to get rid of these parasites. It's like having disposable skin.

Why are frogs slimy?

Next time you struggle to catch your breath after a hard run, imagine how much easier it would be if you were a frog and could breathe through both your lungs and your skin. However, a frog's skin can only absorb oxygen that's dissolved in water. So frogs secrete mucus from glands just below their skin, and the slippery coating keeps water on the skin from drying up. A slimy frog is a healthy frog.

Are there any slimy mammals?

Since hippos live in the tropics they don't need fur, but they do need protection from the water they live in and from the hot sun. To get that protection, they ooze a red, oily, slimy substance from their skin. This helps to prevent the hippo's skin from wrinkling up like a prune when it stays in water for long stretches and from drying out on land.

Bug-Eyed Quiz

1 Some ants are gardeners. They cut leaves and take them to underground chambers, where they use them as mulch to grow fungus.

True ☐   **False** ☐

2 Monarch butterflies feed on poisonous milkweed plants, so birds leave them alone. Viceroy butterflies don't feed on poisonous plants, but birds leave them alone too because they look a lot like monarchs.

True ☐   **False** ☐

3 Insects were the very first creatures on Earth that learned how to fly.

True ☐   **False** ☐

4 A baby dragonfly has gills and can breathe under water.

True ☐   **False** ☐

6 Fireflies aren't really flies, they are beetles.

True ☐   **False** ☐

7 More than half of all living things on Earth are insects.

True ☐   **False** ☐

5 The Hercules beetle from South America is as big as a mouse.

True ☐   **False** ☐

8 Some dragonflies can eat their weight in food every half hour.

True ☐   **False** ☐

9 The South American grasshopper not only looks like a stick but it also sways as though caught in a breeze.

True ☐   **False** ☐

10 Monarch butterflies fly from Canada to Mexico to spend the winter.

True ☐   **False** ☐

11 Only female deerflies bite; males dine on flowers.

True ☐   **False** ☐

12 Houseflies walk all over your food so they can taste it — they've got tastebuds on their feet.

True ☐   **False** ☐

13 Some weevils can drill holes in nuts with their snouts.

True ☐   **False** ☐

14 A bug called the water boatman swims on its back using its paddle-like third pair of legs.

True ☐   **False** ☐

15 Some tropical termites build their mud homes 6 m/18 ft high. An equivalent man-made building would be 4 km/2.5 mi high.

True ☐   **False** ☐

16 The antennae of green male midges act like CB radios, picking up the frequency of buzzing females.

True ☐   **False** ☐

17 One kind of queen termite lives for 50 years and lays 30,000 eggs a day.

True ☐   **False** ☐

18 Some cicadas spend 17 years underground before becoming winged adults.

True ☐   **False** ☐

Answers: All of the statements are true.

Why do drinking glasses slide across the counter when they're wet?

When you place a wet glass rim-side down, hot water runs down its inside and outside surfaces onto the counter. The water in the glass evaporates, changing from a liquid to a gas. Gas molecules take up more room than liquid molecules, so the air pressure increases inside the glass. If the glass isn't too heavy, the gas molecules lift it as they try to escape to the lower air pressure outside. You can see bubbles of escaping air at the glass's rim. Not only does the hot water help lift the glass, it also makes the counter slippery — and zoom! Off goes your glass.

Z o o o m m m m

Why does grease run away from soap?

Next time you're washing dishes, take the greasiest pan you can find and fill it with clear warm water. See the blobs of grease floating on the water's surface instead of sinking and mixing with the water? They can't mix with the water because water molecules cling so tightly to each other that they form a surface "skin," keeping other molecules out. Now drop some detergent on the water in the center of the pan and watch those oily blobs zip away from it. Detergent is specially made to link up molecules of water with molecules of oil. This reduces the clinging power of water molecules so much that the water's "skin" gets a hole in it. The torn "skin" shrinks out to the edge of the pan, carrying the oil with it.

What is a sponge?

A sponge is a very simple animal — it doesn't have a head, a mouth, arms, or legs. Instead it's made up of tiny, microscopic cells that grow very close together. Most sponges live in shallow seas around the world, although a few live in fresh water. Some live alone, others live together in colonies. Some sponges are so small you can barely see them. Some can be larger than a bathtub and others can be up to 2 m/6 ½ ft tall. Some are dull orange or brown, others are bright red or green. Each kind of cell in a sponge has a different job. Some form the skeleton of the sponge and give it its shape, while others serve as protective cells. Some cells stir up the water to make it flow through the sponge, others have holes to allow the water to filter through. Some take in food particles from the water as it flows through, others pass the food to inner cells. And some cells are just for reproduction.

Although most dishwashing sponges are man-made, bath sponges are usually the skeleton of an animal that once lived off the coast of Florida or Greece. Once collected, the sponges are left to dry in the sun so that the soft tissues rot. Then they are pounded and washed, leaving only what's called the spongin skeleton. This skeleton is made up of a network of elastic fibers that can absorb and hold water, and can be squeezed too.

Sponges that don't end up in your bathroom may be eaten by sea slugs, sea stars, turtles and some tropical fishes.

Illustration © Danielle Jones 1989

Why does ice some- times stick to your fingers?

When you pick up an ice cube, heat from your fingers melts a thin layer of ice. If the ice cube is very cold, this layer of moisture quickly refreezes, sticking your fingers to the cube. Most small freezers in the top of refrigerators don't chill ice cold enough to do this, but some freezers can. When metal freezes, the same thing can occur. That's why you need to be careful not to touch frozen metal with your bare hands or tongue.

Why does a newspaper tear smoothly up and down but not from side to side?

Take a close look at a piece of newspaper through a magnifying glass and you'll see that it's made up of tiny wood fibers. If your glass is powerful enough, you'll see that the fibers all line up in the same direction, up and down on the page. This gives the sheet of newspaper a grain, something like the grain in meat. When you tear the newspaper from top to bottom it tears evenly because you're tearing in the direction of the grain. But when you tear it from side to side, it tears unevenly because you're tearing across the grain.

Why do clocks run clockwise?

Mechanical clocks were created in the northern hemisphere by inventors trying to make models of the sun's movement in the sky.

To watch the sun from the northern hemisphere, you have to face south. Then the sun will rise on your left and pass over your head to set on your right. Since the hour hand on a clock was made to follow the sun's motion through the sky, it moves from left to right over the top of the clock —

clockwise. Just think . . . if clocks had been invented in the southern hemisphere, they might run in the opposite direction.

Why do boats have round windows instead of square ones?

When windows were first put in boats about 300 years ago, their frames were cast in bronze and iron. It was easier to spin the metal into a smooth, circular shape on a lathe than to mold it into a square. Also, round portholes — or as sailors call them, portlights — were easier to open and close and could be made watertight. Today, thanks to better metal-working techniques, square portlights are becoming fashionable because they let in more light. Unfortunately, some of them also let in water at the corners.

Do fish sing?

Fish don't actually open their mouths and belt out a tune, but that doesn't stop them from using "fish songs" to communicate with each other. It's true, however, that fish singers are rare: of the 20,000 species of fish only 150 or so species are known to produce high-frequency sounds that we might call "songs."

GOBY FISH

Why do fish sing?

Fish aren't exactly tuneful, so you might well ask why they bother singing at all. Fish are practical creatures, so they don't sing for pleasure (as far as we know). They sing to get a message across, just as birds do. One song might mean "This territory is taken, please move on," another might mean "Time to change direction," and yet another "Let's get out of here." If you're a minnow, a blenny or a goby fish, of course, your song might mean "I'd make the perfect mate for you."

Can you sing like a fish?

Do you grate your teeth? If so, you can already sing like some fish. And if you can also grate your bones together, you can sing a song with a clownfish or a seahorse, because that's how they do it. Others, such as parrotfish, croaking gourami, file-fish and puffers grate all kinds of things — teeth, fins and spines among them.

SEAHORSE

Have you ever made drumming sounds by patting your chest? If so, you can make noises that sound a little bit like the ones triggerfish and several others can make. Each plays its swim bladder "drum" by vibrating muscles that surround it or are attached to it.

W e're not sure how you can ever manage to sing like a barracuda, or a school of herrings, sardines or anchovies. Their sudden movements — a change of direction or swimming speed — create noises that sound like a low roar or a wooden mallet striking a boat underwater.

BARRACUDA

Can you hear a fish sing?

Next time you're out in a boat under the light of a silvery moon, listen carefully. Some fish get together for a night-time sing-song. Marine catfish, for instance, tend to sing together each summer, especially around the time of the new moon. Their chorus, which sounds a bit like a coffee percolator at full boil, starts at 5:00 p.m. and ends at 11:00 p.m. No late show for these ones. Another group of watery wailers, called sea robins, chirp to each other. And if you ever find yourself standing on the shore of any of the Great Lakes, listen for the sounds of freshwater drum fish. What do they sound like? You guessed it . . . drums!

TRIGGERFISH

MARINE CATFISH

Who's the best singer of them all?

It's too bad that the male oyster toadfish can't stand up and take a bow, because he's the star of the fish-singing world, even though he doesn't sing all that often. Since he tends to sing most during the late spring, scientists think that his boat whistle may be a mating call, since he usually makes it at the nest when he's ready to spawn. Although it's the oyster toadfish's boat whistle call that enthralls people and prompts them to compare it to a bird song, that's not the only sound he makes. He's great at grunting too.

What's the loudest hiccup ever heard?

According to the Guinness Book of World Records, in 1769 a man from Long Witton, Northumberland, suffered from hiccups that could be heard more than 1.6 km/ 1 mi away!

What's the quietest hiccup?

Babies can get the hiccups — even before they're born. Pregnant mothers have reported hearing hiccups only to discover that the sound was coming from inside them!

What happens when you get the hiccups?

It's probably happened to you. You're sitting in a quiet classroom and all of a sudden HICC! And then another. HICC! Hiccup after hiccup, and there's nothing you can do, because hiccups are one of those things you can't control. To understand why, you need to know about the workings of your diaphragm.

Your diaphragm is a dome-shaped muscle that stretches across your body between your lungs and stomach. When this powerful muscle contracts, it reduces the air pressure in your lungs so air gets pulled into them — and you inhale. You exhale when your diaphragm relaxes and air is forced out of your lungs. You get an attack of the hiccups when your diaphragm stops behaving normally and goes into a muscle spasm. Being cold can trigger a spasm, and so can having an over-full stomach. Eating and drinking too much can overstretch your stomach so that it presses against your diaphragm. This triggers electrical signals from the nerve that controls the movement of your diaphragm, causing a sudden spasm. Talking while you're eating can also force extra air into your stomach with the same result. So, one way to avoid the hiccups is not to talk with your mouth full.

What's the longest anyone's had the hiccups?

Charles Osborne of Iowa has had the hiccups for more than 60 years. That's approximately 420 million hiccups.

What are the Northern Lights?

The Northern Lights are ribbons of red, pink, and ghostly green light that dance and shimmer for hours across the sky. They occur when the sun bombards Earth with tiny particles of electricity, too small for us to see. When these particles hit the highest part of Earth's atmo-sphere, they electrify the air and make it glow.

Why are the Northern Lights different colors? Each gas in Earth's atmosphere glows with its own color when it becomes charged with electricity. Oxygen gives off an eerie green glow, nitrogen glows red and neon gas turns pink.

Why is a black hole black?

A black hole has such strong gravity that not even a single ray of light can escape. And that means that the black hole can't be seen against the blackness of space. So how do scientists know a black hole is there, you ask? By watching the behavior of stars nearby. Here's how.

If a black hole is in close orbit around a star, gases coming off the star are sucked into the black hole by its gravity. As the gases get pulled in, they get squeezed and heated. When this happens energy is released in the form of gamma rays and X-rays. These rays, which can be detected by scientists on Earth, tell that a black hole is orbiting nearby. Eventually the star will be swallowed up by the black hole.

Why is the moon light and dark when you look at it?

When you look up at the moon parts of it are bright and clear and other parts are shady and dark. Those dark and light markings are caused by mountains and "seas." The seas are not made of water. They're big flat areas of lava that flowed and solidified long ago. Since the lava material is darker than the material that makes up the mountains, the rough mountain areas look light and the large, flat lava plains look dark.

What does it sound like in space?

Sound travels through the air as vibrations. When the vibrating air touches your ear drum and sets it vibrating, you hear the sound. There is no air in space for sound waves to travel on, so space is totally silent.

Why does Earth look blue from outer space?

Earth looks blue from outer space because so much of it is covered with water.

Could people live on Uranus?

Uranus, a massive blue-green ice planet, is a dark mysterious world wrapped in an atmosphere of poisonous methane. At its center is thought to be a rocky core about the size of our planet, surrounded by a slushy methane ocean 20,000 km/12,500 mi deep. Needless to say, it's not a world where humans could live.

Why can't you lift your ring finger when you curl your middle finger under?

It's all a question of tendons. Try this trick. Place your hand on a table in the position shown in the photo.

Try to lift your ring finger. No matter how hard you try, you won't be able to do it. Why? Because the tendons of the middle and ring finger are joined together. When you prevent the middle finger from moving by bending it under, your ring finger can't move either.

Why do you have lines, ridges and swirls on your fingertips?

No matter how young you are, your fingertips and palms are covered with lines and ridges. But don't worry, you need them. They give you a better grip, like the treads on tires. Smooth fingertips would slither off things you're trying to pick up. Prove it by sticking smooth tape over the fingertips of your thumb and index finger. Now try to pick up a piece of paper or a dime or turn the pages of this book . . .

How do artificial hands work?

In this photograph, Jennifer Schoenhals is using a myo-electric hand — a battery-operated artificial hand that she controls with a miniature computer. The computer uses electrical signals from the muscles in her lower arm to tell the hand to open and close, similar to the way your hand works. A gentle muscle contraction closes the hand and a strong one opens it. Her myoelectric hand is easy to remove, so she can quickly switch to her special "swimming" hand, "gymnastics" hand or whatever special-use hand she needs.

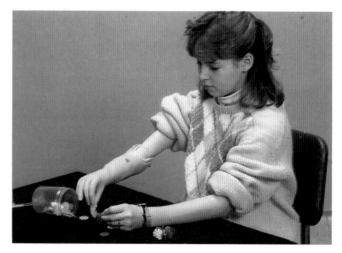

Why do you have baggy knuckles?

Without those baggy knuckles and the loose elastic skin on the back of your hands, you wouldn't be able to make a fist or close your fingers. How much "extra" skin do you need? When you close your hand, the skin distance from the base of your fingers to their tips increases by almost 20 percent. What a stretch!

Why do your thumbs stick out?

Your thumbs are two of the most important digits on your hands, mainly because they're opposable — they stick out separately from your fingers. Without your thumbs you wouldn't be able to shoot a marble, hold a pen, open a jar of peanut butter. . . Don't believe us? If you want to find out how important your thumbs are, tape them to the sides of your hands so you can't use them. Now try to answer the phone, open the door. . .

How come fingers are so strong when they're so small and skinny?

Drum your fingers on a table or "play" the piano in the air. See the "cords" moving in the backs of your hands? Those cords are your tendons, and they attach your muscles to your bones. The tendons in your hands carry muscle power all the way from your elbow to your fingers. So although your fingers might be small and slender, they're backed up by a lot of power.

Why are ants so strong?

Why can an ant lift 50 times its weight while a human weight lifter can't manage 18 times his weight? It's because an ant's body is inside out compared to yours. Your muscles are attached around your bones, but an insect has an outer skeleton with its muscles inside. Its body is made up of hard tubes, and tubes are very strong structures. Unlike many insects, an ant can move its legs to be able to lift things.

Why don't electric eels get electrocuted?

 For the same reason you don't when you move an arm. The electric eel has a set of protective coverings around its nerves that generate the same kind of electricity that you do every time you move a muscle. And just as you are grounded against the electricity you produce, so an electric eel is grounded against its own electri-

city . . . even though it lives in water.

The eel's electric organ runs down the eel's sides. The organ is made up of specialized muscles that can't contract like your muscles. What they can do, however, is work together to discharge electricity.

Normally the eel just puts out a little bit of electricity, which it uses to help it maneuver

around and find food. The electric eel can increase its output for defense. The eel can emit an electric current of 650 volts, enough to stun even a horse.

The electric eel lives in the Amazon basin and is the most dangerous of all electric fish because it can repeat its stunning discharges several times an hour.

Why don't beavers get splinters in their mouths from chewing wood?

Beavers avoid the problem of splinters by never chewing dry wood. They chew down live trees, which are too full of sap to splinter. And in winter they store branches underwater, so these never have a chance of drying out either. Even if beavers did chew on dry wood, they'd still probably never get splinters in their mouths. Their big, furry lips close behind their huge orange front teeth so any splinters would be stopped right there. Beavers can also work very comfortably underwater without getting a single drop of water inside their mouths.

Can you charm a snake?

No, not really — you're just seeing a snake being a snake. When a snake charmer starts to play his flute, the snake, usually a cobra, rises out of its basket to check out the intruder in its territory. When the snake sees the flute player rocking back and forth in time to the music, it does the same. That's because male cobras rise up and follow each other's movements in a "challenge dance" when they meet. The cobra reacts to the snake charmer as if he's a snake. So the flute music isn't important, just the snake charmer's movements.

Why does it hurt so much when you step on something sharp?

Step on a sharp object and bundles of nerves zoom waves of tiny electric shocks from your foot to your spinal column and on to your brain at speeds of 130 m/ 400 ft per second. So there's not much delay between stepping on the object and feeling the pain. Ouch!

But have you ever noticed how quickly you pull your foot to safety? That's because your spinal column has sent a hasty message to your foot telling it to get off the sharp object — fast! So usually you move your foot away before you've really even felt any pain.

How much electricity does your brain need to work?

Your brain is the most complex computer ever . . . but it operates on only 10 watts of electricity. That's the same amount needed to light up one bulb on a string of outdoor lights!

Can you really have a brainwave?

Even when you're asleep your nerve cells are hard at work. They're passing electric shocks all over your brain to keep you dreaming and breathing, and so on. These messages move like waves, and doctors are able to measure them. When you're sleeping, the waves are large and slow. When you're awake but relaxed, they're faster and smaller. And when you're studying or running fast the waves look sharp and jagged. So if anyone ever tells you that a brilliant idea you've had is a "brainwave," just say you have them all the time!

Can the electricity in your body hurt you?

No. In fact, your body's electricity helps injuries heal faster. When you cut yourself, electricity begins to flow from the cut, creating an electric current. This makes nerves in the injured area grow faster and triggers cells to divide and fill in the cut to start the healing process.

Where does the electricity in your body come from?

Your body is made up of millions of tiny cells and those cells need energy . . . electrical energy. How do they get it? They make it from the food you eat. Once food goes into a cell, miniature batteries inside each cell convert some of that food into energy. Around each cell is a membrane. This membrane separates fluids inside the cell from fluids outside the cell. These fluids are different from each other because they contain different electrically charged particles. But when the cell membrane "opens up," the fluids mix together and the electricity flows across the cell wall. How do cells know when to open? When they receive some kind of stimulus. For instance, if someone shines a light in your face, it stimulates the cells in your eyes to produce electricity. The light-sensitive cell membranes produce an electric shock which travels along the nerve to the brain. The brain then forms an image, which you see as the person shining the light on you.

Illustration © Danielle Jones 1989

How do you eat a cactus? ▶

C-a-r-e-f-u-l-l-y. Some-times a land iguana from the Galapagos Islands follows this rule. It carefully scratches off the cactus's spikes so that it can munch on the soft parts. But other times it eats the cactus whole — spikes and all. The iguana must have cast-iron in-sides because the spikes pass right through and are excreted as waste.

Does the vampire bat suck blood?

Forget everything you've heard about Central and South American vampire bats sucking blood from cattle and horses. They don't. They lick up the blood from open wounds. Why doesn't the bat get caught by its prey? First of all, since its feet are padded and it only weighs about 40 g/ 1½ oz, the victim rarely feels the bat land. Also, the bat has razor-sharp teeth to make bites quick and painless. And it only takes about a large spoonful of blood at a time. Being a skilled blood burglar means the bat can come back to the same animal another day.

How many termites does it take to fill up an Australian numbat?

About 20,000 . . . it's no wonder the numbat spends most of its day searching for food. With its strong foreclaws and long tube-shaped tongue, getting termites is a breeze for the nimble numbat. While it gulps small termites and chews on larger ones, the numbat won't pass up a tasty meal of ants. A numbat, by the way, is the only Australian marsupial you'll see sniffing around for food during the day. The others prefer to dine at night.

Do any animals eat porcupines?

In North America, fishers are probably the only animals that make a meal of a porcupine. How do they avoid the quills? They flip the porcupine over so that its soft belly is exposed and it can't fight back. Then they tuck right in.

Sea urchins are a bit like porcupines of the sea. Not many animals will risk eating them for fear of getting a mouth-ful of spines. That's no problem, however, for the sea otters that live off the coast of British Columbia. These nimble-fingered animals pluck off the spines as you might pluck leaves off an artichoke to get at the good stuff inside.

Who's the biggest glutton in the animal kingdom?

The African bullfrog, and most of its cousins, would take the gold medal in this category. It gorges on tasty insects until its stomach is full, its throat is full, even its mouth is full. Sometimes it crams itself so full that tiny twitching insect legs stick out of its mouth.

Who can last the longest without food?

On land, the winner is the North American grizzly bear. It can hibernate for up to seven months without a bite of food by using up stored body fat. But that's nothing compared with the African lungfish. It can live without food or water for more than a year.

Who's the messiest eater?

You wouldn't want to sit next to a starfish at dinner. It pushes its stomach completely out of its body to cover its food. The meal is eaten and digested before the stomach is pulled back in.

1989 1990 1991

Who's the weirdest eater?

When food gets scarce, the ribbon worm eats itself. No, it doesn't take bites out of its own body. Instead it uses up its organs, much the same way as a bear uses up stored body fat.

When food becomes plentiful, the ribbon worm replaces the parts it "ate" and becomes large and healthy again.

Who's the most fearless eater?

This one's a tie. Which do you think should win? The Egyptian plover, which lives along the sandy river banks of Central and Northeastern Africa, nips into the open mouths of crocodiles to feed. Some scientists think it's picking food from the croc's teeth, others think it's gobbling up leeches stuck on the reptile's tongue. The plover is up against a 13 cm/5-inch-long bullfrog that ate a 20 cm/8-inch-long alligator.

Who has the world's biggest appetite for little things?

It's a good thing the blue whale doesn't have to carry home the groceries. This huge mammal stretches as long as three city buses parked end to end. But it feeds entirely on tiny shrimp-like creatures called krill. In the summer, the blue whale fills up on as many as 3.6 tonnes/4 tons of these tiny taste treats a day.

Are there any underwater forests?

If you could take a stroll through this underwater "forest" off the Pacific coast, you'd meet up with many small fish, birds and even sea otters. Why? This dense forest is made up of giant kelp plants. The plants are anchored to the sea floor and their leafy tops float at the surface. Many fish hide from predators in this forest. Harlequin ducks roost on it, and great blue herons use it as a fishing platform. Within the calm inshore water that is protected by the forest, gulls, loons, murres and other seabirds can feed in safety. Even sea otters benefit. They wrap themselves in kelp as a safe anchor while they snooze. And not only does this forest protect all these animals, it also helps calm the seas and protect the shore from surging waves and pounding surf.

What direction would a plant's roots grow in space?

A plant uses gravity to make sure its roots grow down into the soil and its stem grows up towards the sun. Without gravity, the plant doesn't know which end is up, so the roots and stem grow into one big, tangled ball. You can create artificial gravity for plants by growing them in a spinning drum with a light in the center. If you put plants on the inside of the drum, their roots grow towards the outside and their stems grow in towards the light.

How high can sap be lifted up?

The force that raises sap up a tree is strong enough to lift it as high as 110 m/300 ft or more. That's taller than the Statue of Liberty!

How does a cactus get enough water in the desert?

The mighty saguaro cactus is built to beat the desert heat. Old saguaros can stand as tall as a three-story building. But unlike many trees whose roots would be as deep as the tree is tall, saguaros have a shallow root system. A three-story-tall cactus has roots covering an area of 30 m/ 100 ft in diameter and close to the surface so it can absorb rain as fast as it falls. Also, the waxy covering on the saguaro's skin reduces moisture loss by evaporation. Its pleats can expand like bellows as the spongy interior of the plant soaks up water. The moisture from one large rain-soaked saguaro could fill 100 bathtubs.

The saguaro's spines not only ward off would-be nibblers, they also help to break up the winds that rob the plant of moisture. And if a woodpecker drills a nest hole in a saguaro, the cactus seals off the wound with a "scab" to protect itself from water loss.

Why don't planets bump into each other? ▼

They did bump into each other once. The nine planets that circle the sun today are the ones that won the bumping contest.

When our solar system began forming 4.5 billion years ago, swarms of tiny planets, called planetesimals, orbited the sun. Some smashed into each other and became space dust, others collected together to form larger planets. These planets then "absorbed" the planetesimals that ran into them, and grew bigger.

Finally, the nine biggest planets had swept clean pathways for themselves around the sun. And they're still following those bump-free orbits today.

Why is Venus hotter than Mercury when it's farther from the sun?

Mercury, the small planet closest to the sun, has no atmosphere. Venus, halfway between Mercury and Earth, has an atmosphere made up mostly of carbon dioxide that's so dense it hides the planet's surface from sight. Yet the surface of Venus is hot enough to melt lead — hotter even than the daytime temperature of 430°C/ 800°F on Mercury. The reason? The sun's rays can penetrate the thick Venusian clouds and heat the planet's surface, but the heat can't escape back into space. The carbon dioxide acts as an insulating blanket around the planet. So the surface just keeps getting hotter and hotter. Scientists call this the greenhouse effect.

Illustration © Danielle Jones 1989

Why does Saturn have rings?

Scientists believe that Saturn's rings have two causes. First, they think that two of Saturn's moons collided and broke up into pieces. Second, those pieces kept smashing into each other to produce smaller and smaller pieces. That process continued until finally what was left was trillions of pieces of material that now form the rings around Saturn. By the way, if you managed to get hold of one of those pieces and bring it home you'd discover it was made of . . . ice!

Do other planets have sunrises and sunsets?

Yes, but you could see them only on Mercury, Mars and Pluto because these planets aren't shrouded in dense, hazy atmospheres. The length of day differs on all these planets because they rotate at different speeds. Earth rotates once every 24 hours, so the sun sets at the equator 12 hours after it rises. Mercury rotates once every six months! Sunset happens three months after sunrise on this planet. That's a long, hot day — the sun looks three times larger than it does from Earth. A Martian day is almost the same length as ours, but the sun appears one-third smaller. On Pluto, which rotates once every six and a half days, the sun sets three days and four hours after it rises. But since the sun is so far away, it simply looks like a dazzling star in a permanently black sky. A day on Pluto is only as bright as dusk on Earth.

Are there really only seven colors in a rainbow?

Everyone learns the rainbow's colors as ROYGBIV — red, orange, yellow, green, blue, indigo and violet, with red at the top and violet at the bottom.

But the colors don't come in seven clearly marked bands. Each color blends slowly into the next, creating a whole array of subtle colors. And there are at least two bands of color that your eyes can't see. Scientists with special cameras have discovered invisible infrared light above the red band and equally invisible ultraviolet light below the violet band. So ROYGBIV should really become IROYGBIVU!

Why aren't rainbows white like sunlight?

The fact that raindrops can bend light is crucial to the creation of a multi-colored rainbow. Why? Light is made up of many colors, and they all bend differently. Violet light bends more than green, which in turn bends more than red. So when these colors bounce back out of the raindrop, they're all heading in slightly different directions. These differences are small, but they're enough so that by the time the light reaches your eyes, the colors have spread out in the familiar rainbow pattern.

Why can't there be a pot of gold at the end of a rainbow?

Sorry, but it's impossible to find a pot of gold at the end of a rainbow. This isn't necessarily because there is no pot of gold. It has more to do with the elusive nature of rainbows. First of all, a rainbow is a reflection, not a solid object. And secondly, a rainbow is only part of a perfect circle, which of course, has no end. Ah well!

How is a rainbow made?

Rainbows are made out of sunlight and rain. The falling rain forms a sheet of billions of drops of water. Think of this sheet as being like a trick mirror in a midway funhouse — the one with curved glass. The mirror is curved so that the reflection is aimed at one place, which is why you don't see your reflection unless you stand in the right place.

Raindrops act like curved mirrors. Sunlight hits the raindrops, bounces once inside them and is reflected out. But it doesn't come out helter-skelter. It's concentrated at a particular angle, almost like a flashlight beam. When you look at the right place in the sky, you see each beam of light from all those raindrops coming together to make a rainbow.

Why do ski jumpers almost touch their noses to their skis when they're soaring through the air?

Leaning forward at that uncomfortable-looking angle helps a skier jump farther. Air flows faster over the curve of his back than below him, and faster-moving air means less air pressure. That creates lift, which helps the jumper stay in the air longer and so travel farther.

How do skiers know which wax to put on their skis?

Before skiers can put wax on their skis they must first check the temperature and snow conditions to know which wax to apply. Here's why they need to know. All snowflakes have six pointed arms. But old snowflakes, or "warm" snowflakes, have lost the points on their arms. For a skier to get a grip on this kind of slippery snow, she needs to use a soft wax so that the snow-flake's shortened arms can poke into it and take hold. New or "cold" snowflakes have longer, sharper arms, so they stick to wax a lot more easily. Using a hard wax ensures that this dry snow won't stick to the skis too much and slow the skier down.

Why do downhill racers use oddly bent poles?

t has to do with streamlining. The curve in those poles allows them to wrap closely around the skier's waist to reduce the slowing effect of the air he has to race through. And the special covers on the baskets at the ends of the poles direct the air around him and steady him. The skier further streamlines himself by zooming down the hill with his back almost parallel to his skis, elbows tucked inside his knees, head pulled in and hands near his chin. It's fondly known as the "egg position."

How did sheep survive the heat before people sheared them?

Very well, thanks to their thick, fleecy wool that keeps out not only the cold but the heat too! Even on the hottest day the wool close to a sheep's skin can be more than 11°C/20°F cooler than its outer wool. Why else do sheep need fleece? It's loaded with oily lanolin, so rain runs off the top layer the way water runs off a duck's feathers.

Why don't mountain sheep slip?

Leaping from boulder to boulder on steep mountain slopes isn't at all scary for mountain sheep. Their hooves are split into two toes that can spread apart and grip uneven surfaces. On the bottom of each hoof is a soft pad that helps absorb the impact of hard landings and gives the sheep a non-slip contact with the ground. Although most domestic sheep no longer leap around mountain slopes, they still have the same split hoof as their wild relatives.

Why do sheep follow the leader?

You may think sheep are stupid because they are always ready to follow the leader. Yet following a leader makes sense if you're a sheep. In the wild, there's safety in numbers, and older sheep can also show young ones where to find the best food.

Why do some sheep's horns curl?

A sheep's horns curl because of the way they grow. Usually the outside surface of the horn grows more quickly than the inside, so the horns curl under. How fast the horns grow depends on the sheep's diet. If there's lots of food to munch on, the horns grow more than in a lean year when there's not much food. By the way, to tell the age of a sheep you count the number of rings on its horns. Telling its age is not what a sheep uses its horns for, though. Males use them to determine who's the leader and to attract a mate. Females use them for defense.

What's a scab?

Skateboarders call scabs pavement pizzas, but you might prefer to think of them as bandages your blood makes. Here's why. When you scratch or cut yourself, cells in your blood instantly start a two-part patching process. They stick around the edges of the cut to help plug up the wound and at the same time produce a substance that makes a protein called fibrin. When seen through a microscope, fibrin looks like strands of spaghetti. As the strands form, they interweave and slowly pull together the sides of the wound. Blood cells get trapped between the fibrin strands, turning the scab dark red.

Why does it hurt so much when you hit your funny bone?

The funny thing about your funny bone is that it's not a bone at all. What you're really hitting is your ulnar nerve, the nerve that carries messages to and from your brain and fingers. Most of your nerves are well protected by skin and flesh. But for some reason — and scientists aren't sure why — your ulnar nerve doesn't have much padding where it passes through your elbow. So when you bump your elbow, you often hit the nerve — OUCH! Not only does it really hurt, it also sends that weird tingly feeling to your fingers.

Why do bruises start off black and end up yellow?

Ouch! You bruise yourself when you break tiny blood vessels beneath your skin. But your body soon repairs the damage. Within minutes blood vessels reseal and clean-up cells arrive to break down and carry away the dead, leaked blood cells. This blood looks black and so your new bruise looks black. As more dead blood cells are removed, the bruise gets lighter in color and looks blue. After a few black-and-blue days your bruise looks green because some molecules in the dead blood turn green as they're broken down. As more of those molecules are carted away, your bruise turns lighter green or yellow, until it disappears.

Why does it hurt to bend your knee after you've scraped it?

Once you've scraped your knee it will start to scab. Not only does a scab look different from the rest of your skin, it also isn't as stretchy and elastic. So when you bend your knee, the scab doesn't stretch. Instead it pulls against the sensitive edges of the scraped area. And that hurts!

Do animals have to take baths?

If you think this rhinoceros will need a bath after it's finished playing in the mud, think again. Why? It's actually wallowing in the bath this very moment. This might not look like a good way of getting clean to you, but mud wallowing gets rid of ticks and flies and cools the animal off. As a bonus, the mud coating protects the rhino's skin from the sun's harmful rays.

A giraffe has other ways of keeping clean. Since it isn't very easy for a giraffe to lie down to bathe, it relies on the rain to wash the dust of the African savannah out of its coat. And it depends on a little bird to pick out the ticks that get embedded in its hide. It's not unusual to see several tick birds, or oxpeckers, hard at work searching for insects on a giraffe's neck.

How does a snake stay clean?

The rat snake doesn't have to worry about staying clean. Although it spends all its time crawling around on the dirty ground, grime doesn't cling to its smooth skin. Even if it did, it wouldn't matter. In order to grow, snakes must shed their skin. So, about once a month, the snake sheds its old, dusty skin, emerging with a gleaming clean one. It even sheds its eye-coverings! As it sheds, the discarded skin is turned inside out. Lizards and other reptiles also keep clean by shedding their skin. It's a bit like throwing away all your clothes when they get dirty.

Do fish ever get dirty?

Even though fish swim around in water, they need an occasional clean-up too. In warm tropical seas, cleaner shrimp keep other fish clean by deftly nibbling off parasites. They also clean wounds. Even when the cleaner has to dig out parasites from below the skin, its fishy clients remain motionless. They even allow the shrimp into their gill covers and mouths. Talk about getting into your work!

Why does my dog bark when I play the clarinet?

No offense meant, but your clarinet might sound like a howling dog. If so, your dog will instinctively bark and howl back. It's just good dog manners to do that.

Or perhaps you have trained your dog to bark without meaning to. For instance, if he starts to bark just as you begin to play the clarinet or when you hit a wrong note, you probably pay attention to him by laughing or patting him. By doing this, you reward him for barking. If the same thing happens again, your dog will quickly learn to howl when you play the clarinet. He figures he'll get lots of attention if he does!

How can cats lick dirt off their fur without gagging?

Although you'd probably gag at the thought of licking yourself clean every night, it doesn't bother a cat at all. Perhaps it has to do with the fact that cats have different taste buds than you do. You probably don't lick your lips when you see a dish of raw liver, but your cat will wolf it down and look for more. And a cat will likely turn up its nose at things that you consider treats — like cookies and cakes. If your cat licks you, she might like the salt on your skin.

Does my goldfish drink water?

Your goldfish drinks water, but not through its mouth. Instead, it absorbs water through its gills and skin. Watch a goldfish when it's feeding and you'll see that it tries to take in as little water as possible through its mouth. This is to prevent its blood — which has more salt in it than the surrounding water — from becoming diluted with fresh water. The fish absorbs the salt from the water as the water passes across its gills during breathing. Then it pumps out the excess water it doesn't need.

Saltwater fish, of course, have the opposite problem. Because there's so much salt in the water around them, they gulp down all the water they need through their mouths. Then they get rid of the salt through their gills or with their body wastes.

Why does my budgie mumble to itself?

Put several budgies together and they'll mutter, chirp and mumble all day long. They're no doubt communicating with each other, although it's difficult to tell what they're saying when they mutter. Chances are your budgie is a sociable little bird who's mumbling to you as if you were another budgie. If you've got a lone budgie for a pet, perhaps you should consider getting it a companion. Or perhaps you could just mumble back!

Why do you sink in quicksand?

On the surface quicksand looks like solid ground. But it's really a pit filled with water and loose wet sand. If you weigh more than an ant and you step on quicksand, you'll sink because the water can't support your weight. The deeper you sink, the more sand there is in the water to weigh you down. If you get caught in quicksand, don't panic. Lie flat on your back and spread out your arms and legs. You'll float to safety.

On a hot day, why does a long asphalt road look like it has water on it?

You might find it hard to believe, but that puddle of water down the road is really a reflection of the sky. What is it reflected by? The road? No, by a "mirror" formed by bent rays of light. Light waves travel faster through cooler air. When light rays from the sky reach the hot air rising off a hot black road, they bend. At the point where they bend, the light rays act like a mirror reflecting an image of the sky. The image is known as a mirage. And sometimes, a mirage can be upside down. For example, at sea the layers of air near the water can focus light waves from a ship into an upside-down image in the sky. So if you see an upside-down ship on the horizon, don't call the coast guard. It's merely a mirage.

Why do you have to punch two holes in a large juice can to let the juice out?

It has to do with vacuums — spaces without gases, liquids or solids. When juice leaves the can, air rushes in to replace it or else a vacuum forms where the juice used to be. When you pour from a can with just one hole in it, you get a squirt of juice and then nothing but a "glug glug" sound as air is sucked in through the hole. You have to wait until the space left by the squirting juice fills with air before you get more juice. But if you punch two holes in the can, air goes in one hole as juice flows freely out the other one.

What's a googol?

A dripping faucet? A big number? A large gull-like bird? If you chose "a big number," you're right! A googol is a big number and we're not talking about a mere 1,000,000. A googol is a number written as "1" followed by 100 zeros. And if a googol is not a big enough number, there's a googolplex as well. That's a googol times a googol. Mind-boogling!

73

Why can't I sleep with my eyes open?

You have two muscles that control your eyelid, one that holds it open and one that closes it. When you sleep, the muscle that closes the lid is more active. It's a good thing, too. Your brain needs a break from the endless flow of pictures it has to process while your eyes are open. But, most importantly, by keeping your eyes closed when you sleep, you keep them moist. The sensitive, delicate covering of your eye, the cornea, needs to be constantly moistened by tears. If it dries out, you won't be able to see.

Why can I curl my tongue but my friend can't?

Curling your tongue is something that you inherited through your genes. Check out your family. Can either or both of your parents curl their tongues? How about your grandparents? Someone among your ancestors was able to perform this trick and they passed it on to you.

Why do we have wax in our ears?

You may not like having wax in your ears, but it's there for a good reason — it keeps your ears in good working order.

Wax is produced by glands near the eardrum and continually washes away down the ear canal. One of the most important things wax does is protect the eardrum from bacteria. It also keeps the eardrum moist and pliable so that it can respond to different sounds.

And if that's not enough to make you glad about wax, then what about this? Earwax also prevents dust and bugs from getting stuck in your ears!

Why do you get bad breath in the morning?

Bad breath is a reminder that your body is active even as you sleep. During the night, your stomach churns because you haven't eaten for a while. Smelly stomach gases rise up through your throat. When you open your mouth the next morning — jungle breath! Also as you sleep, skin inside your mouth that's slowly rubbed away hangs around and creates smelly fumes. And if you forgot to brush your teeth the night before, decaying food will also cause bad breath.

INDEX

PHOTO and ILLUSTRATION CREDITS

CONSULTANTS